WILD ANIMAL
PORTRAITS COLORING BOOK

Llyn Hunter

DOVER PUBLICATIONS, INC.
Mineola, New York

In this exquisite coloring collection, you'll find thirty-one beautiful renderings of wild animals from all over the world. The latest addition to Dover Publications' *Creative Haven* series for the experienced colorist, the highly-detailed illustrations offer ample opportunity for experimentation with color and technique, and the perforated, unbacked pages make displaying your finished work easy!

Copyright
Copyright © 2015 by Dover Publications, Inc.
All rights reserved.

Bibliographical Note
Wild Animal Portraits Coloring Book is a new work, first published by Dover Publications, Inc., in 2015.

International Standard Book Number
ISBN-13: 978-0-486-79176-0
ISBN-10: 0-486-79176-9

Manufactured in the United States by LSC Communications
79176907   2020
www.doverpublications.com

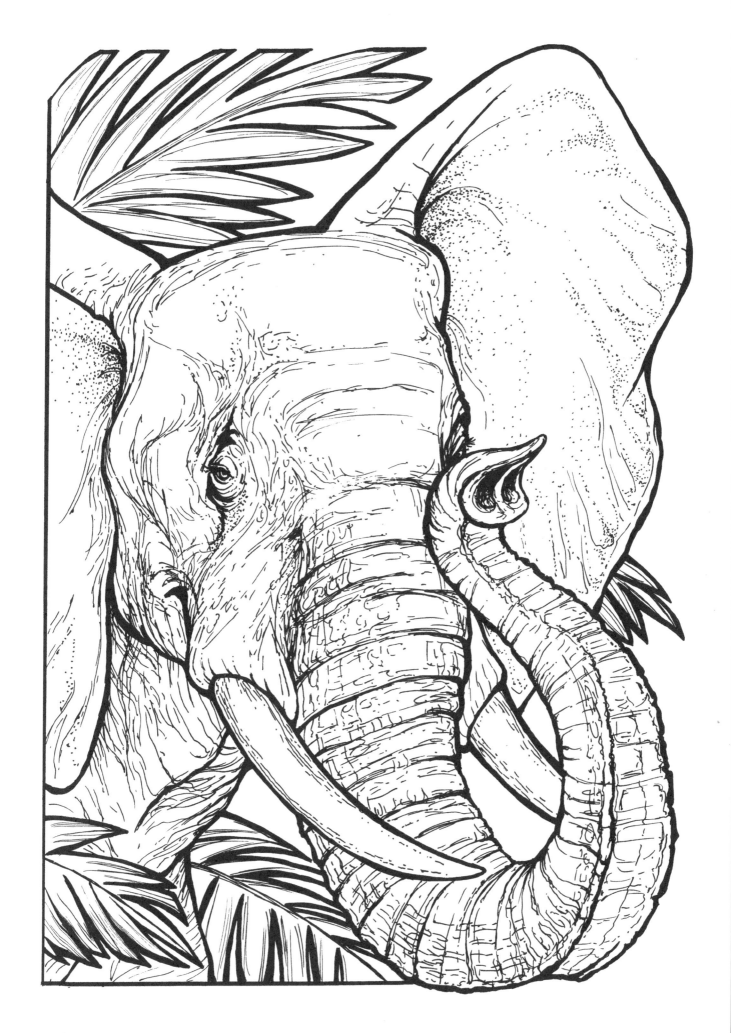

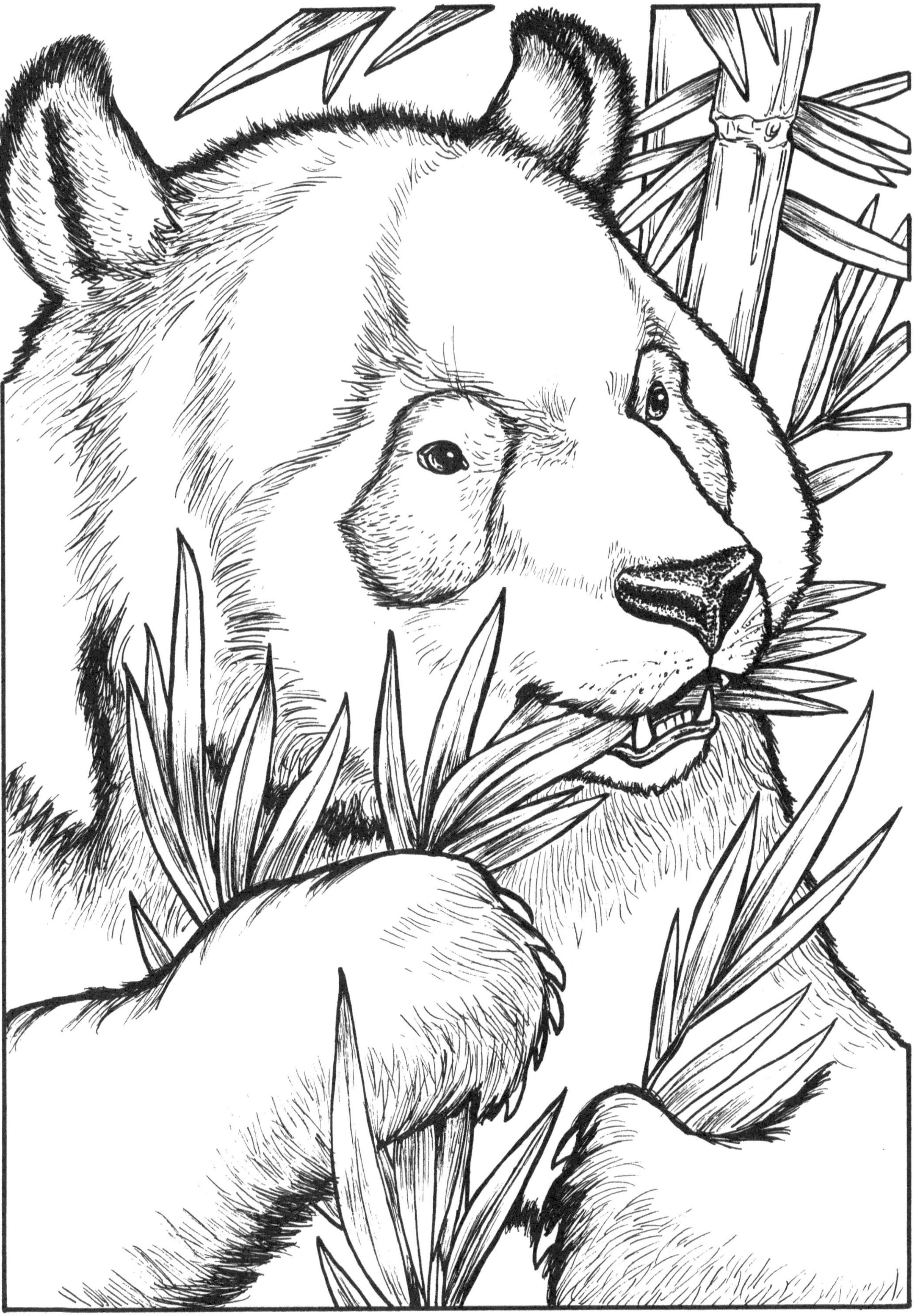

6. White Rhino (*Ceratotherium simum*). Africa.

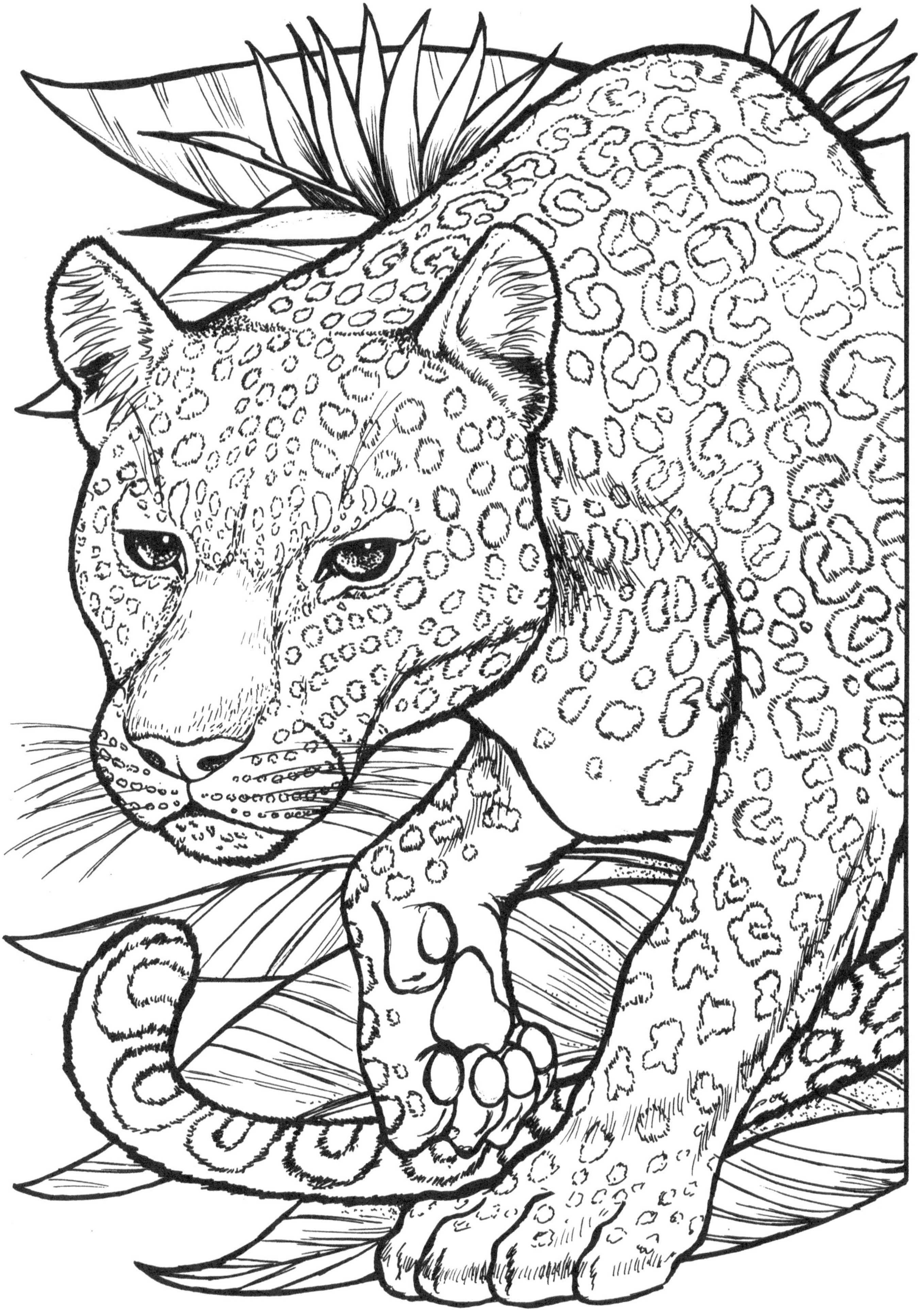

11. Leopard (*Panthera pardus*). Asia/Africa.

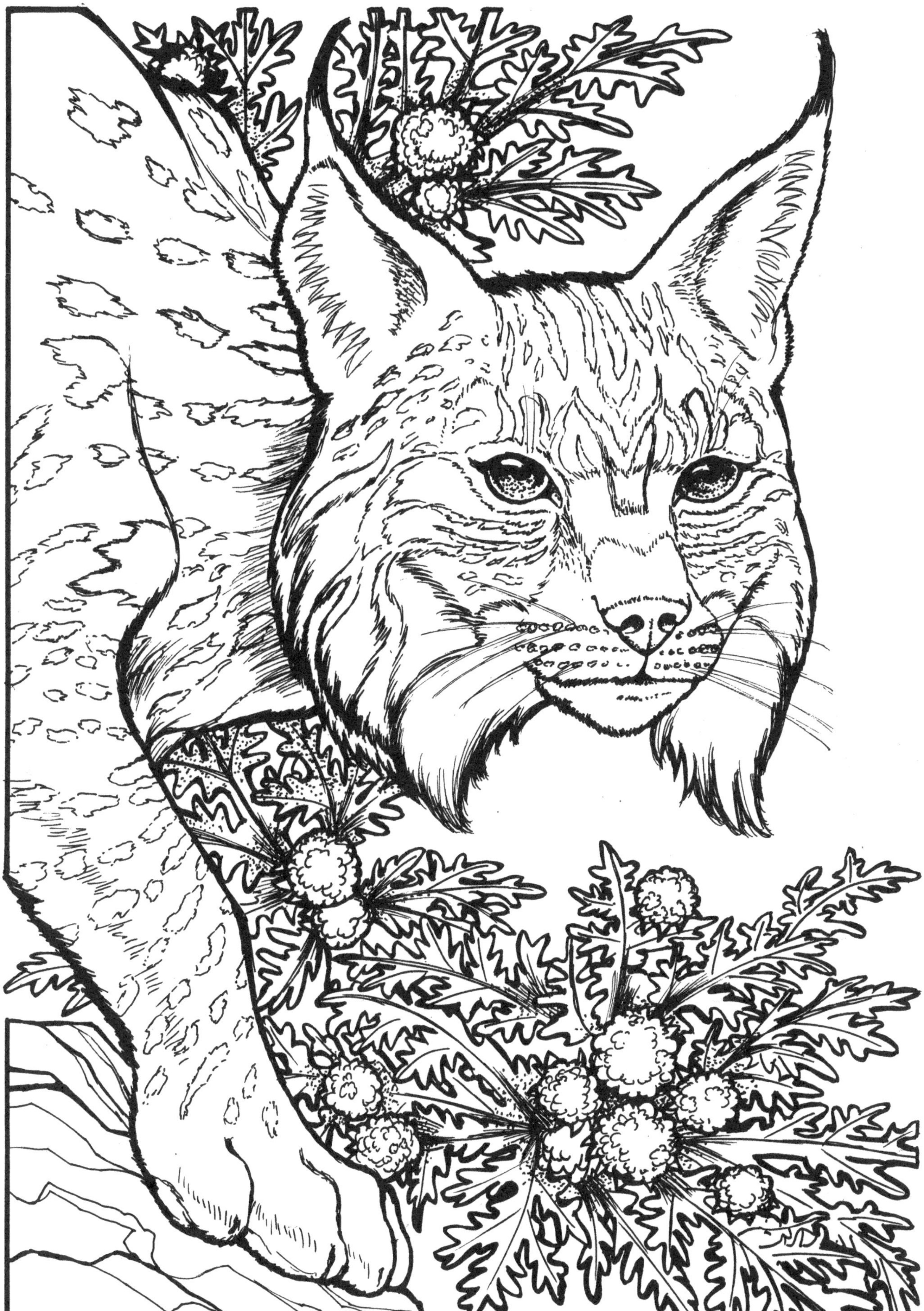

13. Lynx (*Lynx lynx*). Europe/Asia.

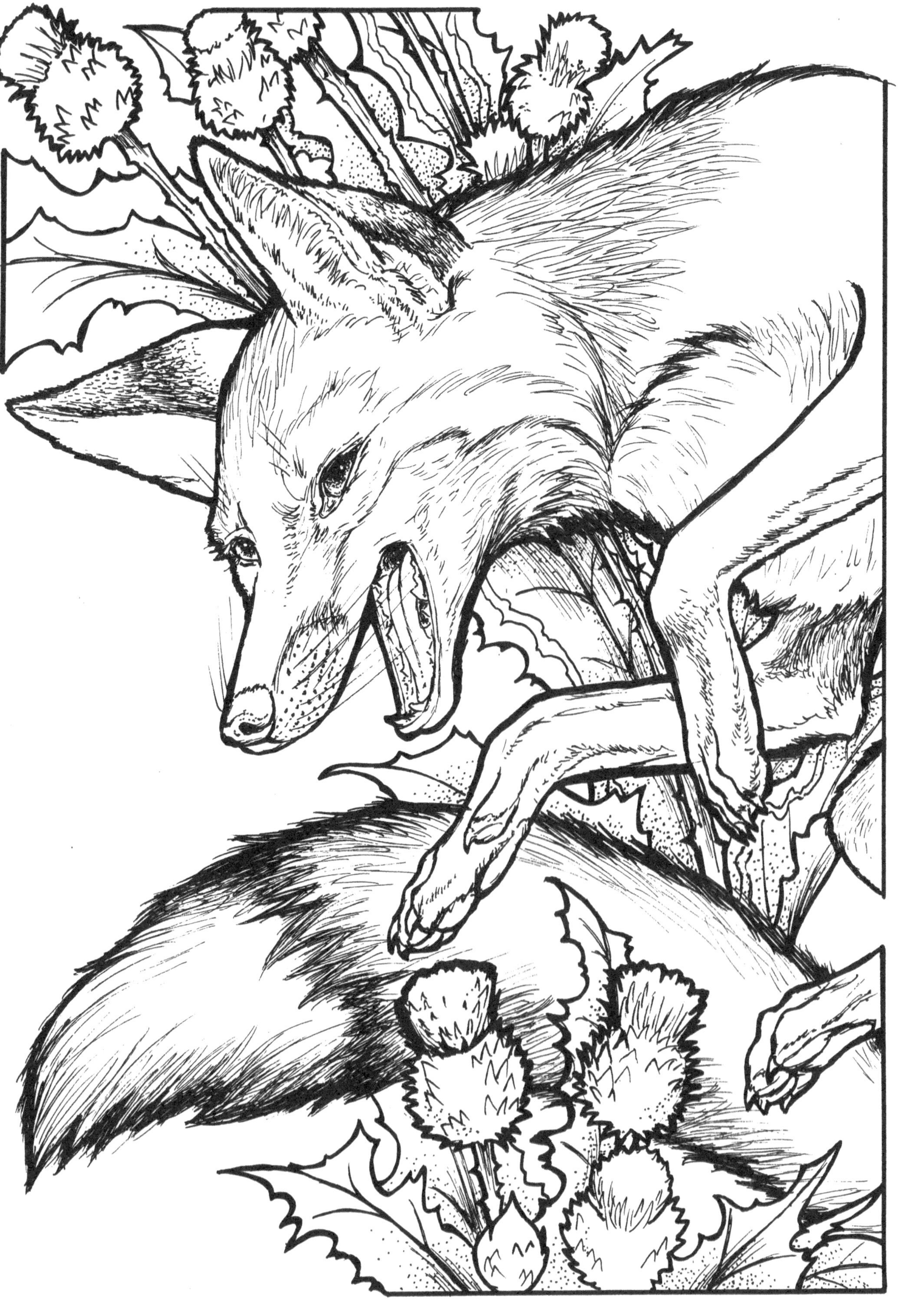

15. Red Fox (*Vulpes vulpes*). Europe/Asia/Africa/North America.

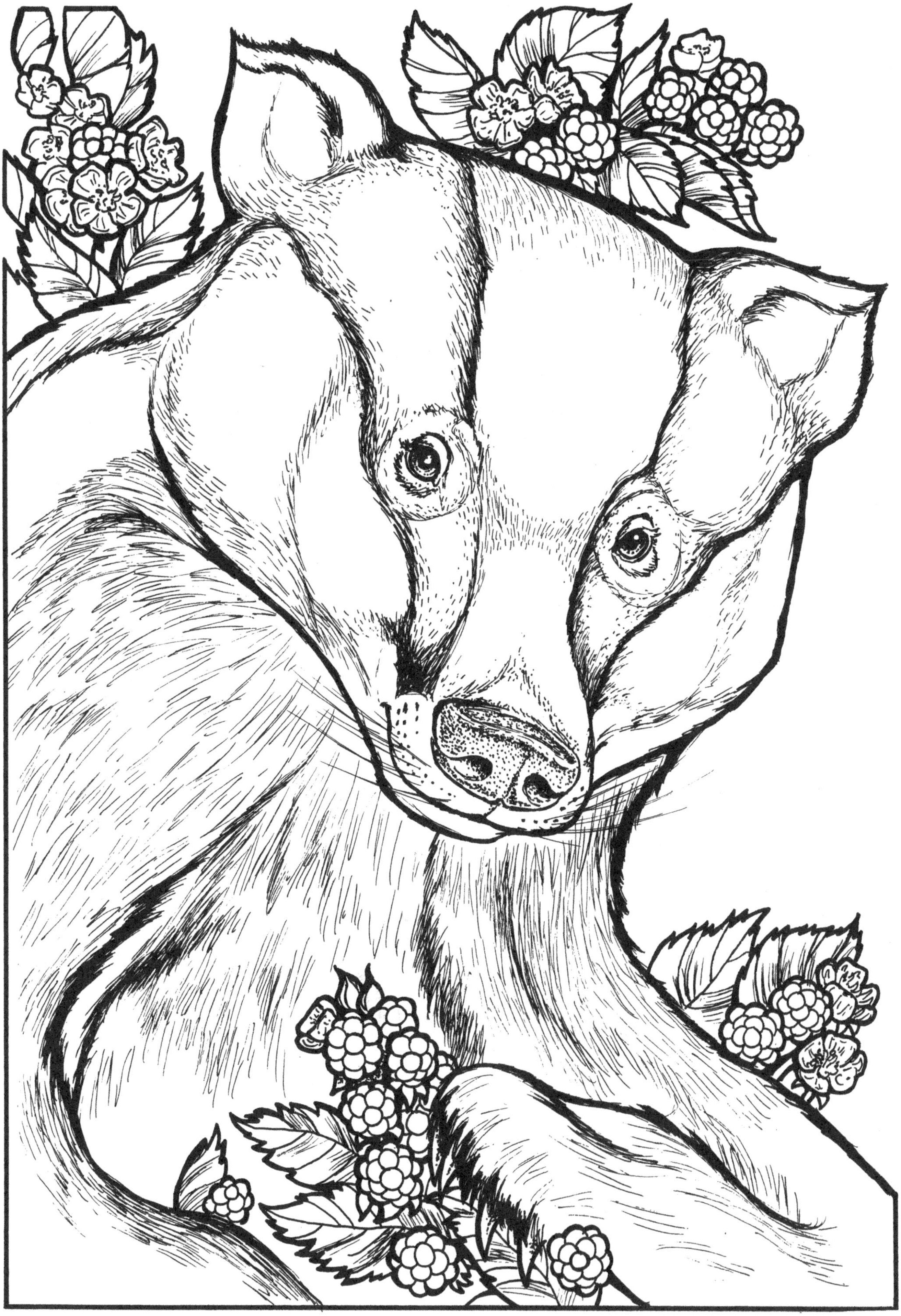

16. European Badger (*Meles meles*). Europe.

17. River Otter *(Lontra Canadensis)*. North America.

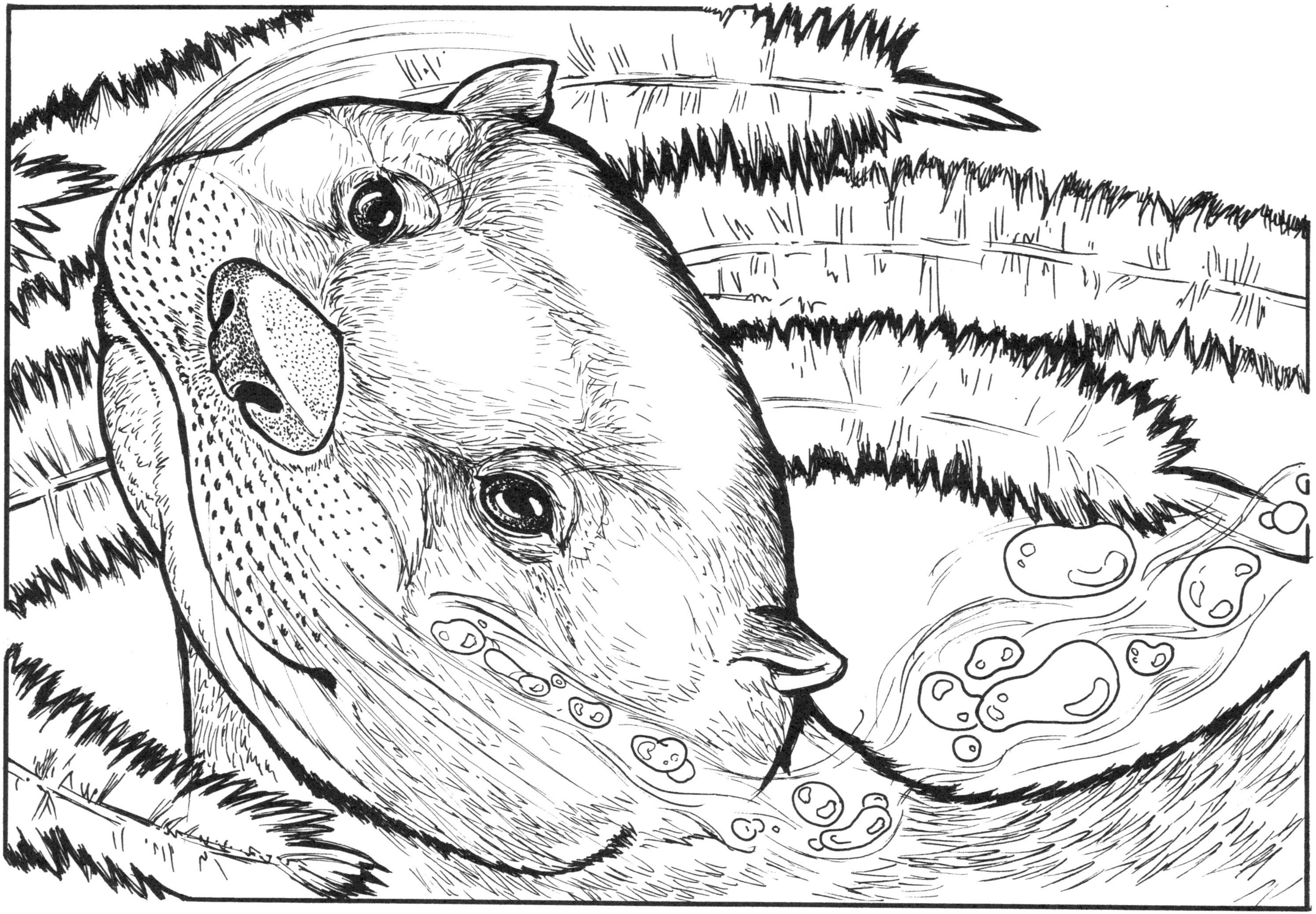

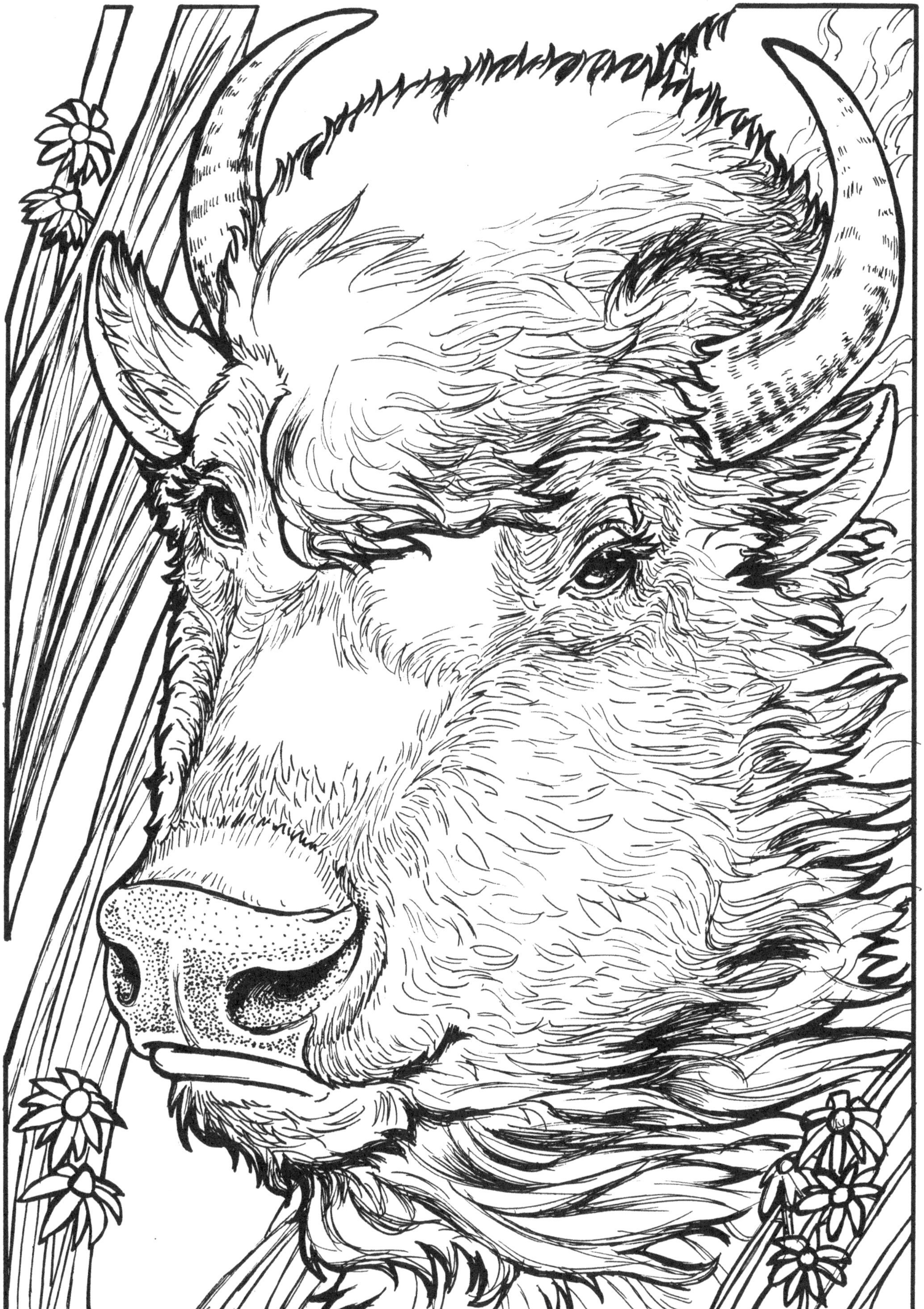

25. Bison (*Bison bison*). North America.

29. Llama (*Lama glama*). South America.

28. Sea Lion (*Zalophus californianus*). Northern Pacific/Mexico.